FREEDOM

I0428982

PARADISE

BY: SCHOLARLY ACTIVISTS

Table of Contents

Walking

By HA

Walking down the mountain in a line

Sweating and gasping all around

Sleeping in the dark with insects you couldn't see

Up the mountain down the mountain

Up the walls down wall

America here we come!

INTRODUCTION

By: SS

At first these stories crushed my heart into millions of pieces because letting it out is not easy. It's full of sympathy mixed emotions, IT'S AN AMERICAN DREAM!!!!!! To turn it into a reality is what the American Dream is.

Our stories are told in historical passages, in rooms where the elder gather with the younger. And now, it will be told here, in this anthology. It will show the suffering our elders endured to pass the border, either passing by bus, plane, boat, or foot, trying to get to their final destination: The Promise Land!

While coming to the United States some got diseases, while others starved, or had to give up their children so they can eat well and they wouldn't die at a young age. Sacrifices were made. Somewhere teenagers looked for a better life to live in, to survive, to find a better life.

Parents do not often tell their stories of how they immigrated; it's mostly a secret to them, hidden deep down dark in their heart. That's just one piece of sacredness feeling as they can't express how they feel for it's like losing someone in your life without knowing who they are and that's an enemy which you never take out of your heart, it's a feeling no one wants to feel but one day they will ask themselves, "Should I pass on my own sad story to my child? Should I tell them about all the sacrifices I made just to move from one place to another?" Should I tell them how difficult it was and that some people even died attempting it?" These are the battles our elders must face before they could even share these stories with us. These are the stories that are collected here, told, listened to, written down, but never forgotten.

Florida

BY: MD

In Miami, Florida there is always sun shine, usually rain, but not a lot of Hispanics. Living in Florida there was once a family with two kids, a four year old, and an eleven year old. They lived in a home with only two small rooms and one kitchen and one bathroom.

The father had to give one room to the kids and the other to the mother for her rest. "Soon, my little ones, we shall get better homes, better rooms, better food, and better lives," he promised them.

The boys trusted their father, who has helped them through all the bad times. "Okay, papa, we will help you through your struggles and one day we will enjoy life together," they said.

They made their father smile with hope.

Six years passed and the boys grew older, one was now a ten year old and the other was a seventeen year old. Now, the boys could help their father with the challenges they faced.

"Father, can I help with the house bills from now on?" Asked the oldest.

"You may, but with what money?"

"Papa, I have dropped out of school in order to help you with the taxes."

The father had no idea what to say to him. He was shocked by this.

"Papa, are you okay?" He asked.

"Why,why did you do this?"

"Because you are the only one here that works, always bleeds out, always cries for help, but never gives up or lets us down. It is because of you that we have never lived on the streets cold, lonely, scared, hungry. You need help, sometimes you have to accept that you need the help"

The father cried himself to sleep that night, thinking, "Why did my son do that for me?"

The night was as cold as the polar ice caps and the family had sheets as thick as a shirt. Shivering all night long, unexpectedly the older son left the house and went to a job interview. He got the job, but they told him that he had to drive across the country, to the other side of the world.

"I'll think about it,' 'he said and walked away.

The next morning he told him"papa everything. '

"Yes!" Papa replied, "Yes, yes, yes!"

"If I work that far away then I may not see you for a long time,Said the son.

"But at least you will not be stealing," said the father.

And the boy, he went back to the men and accepted the job and soon moved far, far from his family. He saved as much money as he could and sent it back to his family. But he missed them very, very much and realized that his family meant more to him than anything else in the world and their absence hurt him like an open wound. So he saved enough to move them across the vast distance, to a new land, a land of hope, a land where dreams can come true.

Mexico

By: OS

Mexico is really busy. It is also dangerous. People die there with family members. People and kids immigrate because they don't want to be the next death.

In the city of Chiapas, Mexico it is really busy. It is filled with people, kids, and babies, all dying of hunger. Mice scattering through the homes and streets and parks, searching for food, but there is no food. Ants walking on kids and babies. Imagine what life would be like if it were you?

In Mexico lived a young girl named Emily. She lived in the streets with her Mom and Dad. The problem is that the people move them from street to street. Nobody wants them on their street but they still need a street to call home.

They were tired of moving, sad and tired. They also did not have any money, food, and shelter. Then Emily said, "Can we immigrate to the UNITED STATES?"

But, the dad said, "No!" He did not want to leave his home. He would miss the streets and the mice.

But, the mom said, "Ok," because she was tired of both.

But ,the dad would not listen to her and he continued to say, "NO!" Still!

So, Emily asked her dad, "Do you want to live a free life?"

The dad thought about this for a long time and finally said, "Yes, yes, I do."

"So why don't you want to immigrate?" Asked Emily.

Then the dad said, "You are right, we need to go to the UNITED STATES!"

So the family started to pack up their possessions and the next day, they started their long trip!

How My Mom Survived

By: Maria De Los Angeles

My mom is nice and that's why I love her. I appreciate her for doing everything for me. If my mom wouldn't protect me, I wouldn't be here right now. She lived in a dangerous place in El Salvador.

There was an earthquake there long ago and my mom panicked. She thought she would of die there. Before the house was torn into pieces she grabbed a suitcase that had what she needed to survive. In that suitcase there was money, it was $100,000,000.

When the shaking stopped for a bit, everyone ran out of the house. Those that couldn't get out of the house died when the house collapsed. After that, my mom turned to my uncle saying "This is it, I am going to the U.S."

"Count me in!" said, my uncle.

"Okay then we are going to the United States," said my mom. And that is how it all began.

My mom and uncle started their journey to the United States. They were 15 years old when they came. My mom was 20 and pregnant. I came out a few weeks later. There was a man who wanted to take me away. The man said, "give me your baby or your life will be in danger."

"I will never give you my baby and my life will not be in danger!" my mom said. She didn't know who he was, maybe he was just crazy, but his words she carried with her on her journey.

She came to learn English. She came for a better life. She came for me. She traveled by foot. There was a beach, it was beautiful, it was at night. The reflection of the moon was casting light on the ocean. It was peaceful; you could hear the ocean crashing against the sand.

Then the helicopter was hovering over the ocean, looking to see if there were any people crossing the border. There were palm trees everywhere. My mom and uncle hid under a palm tree. The helicopter was close; it had a light so bright it seemed as if you were looking right at the sun. If someone moved a branch or a muscle LA Migra would find him or her!

The people didn't move at all. My mom crumbled like a coat, she was scared of getting caught. In a dangerous country of El Salvador my family was huge, but now there was only the three of us and we were feeling as if we were all alone and lost.

The helicopter did not see us and in the darkness we continued.

My mom survived by drinking water. She had walked a lot with a group of people. She had fainted and called my uncle over. She had cuts on her feet.

"I don't feel good just go," she had told my uncle. "Leave me here."

"No, I'll carry you there if necessary. I will never leave you here" my uncle said. And he meant it.

When we arrived, she didn't have a place to stay so she called my aunt. My aunt had come to America before my mom. "Hey, sister can you come to pick us up?", my mom asked.

"Oh my God, you are here in the U.S?", my aunt said surprised and happy. My aunt met her. They were happy to see each other again. My aunt said, "Sister, if you want, you could live with me."

"Okay, thank you", my mom said and we all moved in.

Two years passed. My mom finally got a job. She also found a place to live, our own place. She tried not to talk to people. She tired not to make friends. She was scared that somebody would find out and send her back.

When a stranger went up to her at her new job and asked if she was new, she said, "Yes I am new. Now, if you will excuse me, I will like to go back to work."

Weeks passed, when someone called my mom, she was terrified, wondering who was calling. She answered, "Hello who is this?"

"It is the guy you work with," said the voice.

After they were done talking. She hung up. My mom received another "Unknown" call, but she didn't answer. The person who called left a voicemail, saying, "Your mother is in the hospital, you have to come back to Salvador to see her,"

My mom immediately called my cousin Brian "Is my mother okay? Is she in the hospital? I just got a strange call from a man that said I have to come back because she is in the hospital. Why is she in the hospital!", she said with fear.

"Calm down, she is okay and she is not in the hospital, why in the world would you think that?" my cousin Brian asked.

"I had received a call that she was in the hospital and said to come back to Salvador", my mom said.

"No don't listen to who ever called you, it is a trap!" cousin Brian said with fear. "If anything happens, we will let you know. Plus she is trying to come to you. She misses you guys."

Months passed, and I was getting older and we were happy. We forgot about the man trying to take me away from my family and all the evil men in the world. We forgot about the strange phone calls and started to enjoy life, we started to hope for the future. We thought he was far away, in El Salvador and we were here, safe in the United States.

One day, my family and I went to eat and we saw the ma. He had followed us to the United Sates and he tried to grab me again. But there was a security guard that saw the man. The security got the man and called the cops, and the cops came and arrested the guy.

A few months later my mom wanted her own mom to come to the United States. We had spent a lot of money for her to come. She spent more than $13,900.

My grandmother had an appointment with the government. She wanted permission to come. She was too old to sneak across the border. But two days before her appointment, my grandmother fell and split her head open.

My mother was scared, she sent a lot of money to pay for her hospital bills and get her therapy. My grandmother never walked again. Five months past my grandma had the appointment with the government again this time she went. The government told her that she was allowed to come to the United States.

My family and I were happy that she was coming. On December 6, 2015 my family and I went to get her. We left at 9 we got there at 10 and my grandma was going to get there at 10:30 but the flight came late.

It was almost midnight when we saw her. When we saw her we all started crying because we had gone a long time without seeing her. We were so glad that she was finally with us. Our family was together again and that is what matters in life! We learned a lesson that day that family is important and to never let go of the good memories you have with your family.

The Forgiving

By: HE

When I was born I was happy because when I first opened my eyes I saw both of my parents. I went home, but I couldn't walk, so my dad had to carry me. My dad was saying words to me, but I didn't know what he was saying. I was a little scared because I didn't know what was happening.

A couple of years passed. When I was seven, my mom and dad got into a fight. My mom accidentally dropped my dad's coat and found out that he had drugs. I was in my room and I heard my mom crying, so I went downstairs and I hid in the side of the hallway and heard them arguing.

Mom said, "Why do you have this? You can go to jail for this, so just get out of here."

Dad said, "Fine, I will leave."

So my dad left for three months. I thought he was never going to come back. I was alone because my mom worked and I was alone till my mom came back from work around 6 PM. I stayed home with my brother but he was always in his room, so I just stayed in the living room and watched TV. The living room was kind of big. We had three couches, one on either side of the room and one in the middle back. They were all facing the TV, which was in the front. It was the most important thing in the room.

Three months passed by between when he left and when my dad came back. My mom talked with my dad about what happened.

My mom had her hands on her waist. She had her left foot tapping on the ground. Mom asked, "Where were you? And where did you stay? We were worried."

Dad said, "I was in a hotel in Hollywood I paid only 50$ a month."

Mom said, "Ohhh, okay." She didn't know what else to say so she repeated herself, "We were worried about you."

He said nothing for a while.

Then Mom said, "We thought you were never going to come back. "

Dad said, "Of course I was going to come back. I don't want my kids to grow up without a dad. I want to see them growing up. I'm never going to let them grow up without me."

I was hiding in the bathroom, scared, excited, nervous, and confused. I kept quiet and listened. I thought, "You liar! You left us for three months and didn't even visit or send a note!" I thought he didn't care about my mom, my brother, or me.

My parents talked about it for a long time and eventually, they worked things out. In the end, I was so happy that my dad came back. And I finally, after many months, I forgave my dad.

My parent's worked hard, saved up and bought a new house, far from where we had lived and I had to leave and go to another school. I was happy because I made new friends and our family got to start over again. The place I used to live in looked like an old abandoned store. So, we left it all behind, all the brokenness and moved somewhere beautiful.

The lesson I learned was what ever starts bad, ends good! Time and actions can change anything and that people who do bad things will eventually do something to be forgiven. So forgiveness does happen.

The Story of my Life

BY: MN

One day, when my mom came back from work, her parents weren't home. When she was going to sit down on the bed, her brother came up and told her that their dad was in the hospital.

"Oh my goodness! What are we going to do?" Said my mom.

"How many weeks will he be there? What's wrong with him?" She asked. My uncle told my mom, "He is going to stay in the hospital for two weeks."

Two weeks later, my mom saw her dad. She was so grateful to see her dad again. When her dad came home he was sitting in a wheelchair. She thought, *'what is going to happen to my dad? Will he never walk again?'*

When she went to her room she locked herself in, sat down on her bed, and she started crying! When she stopped crying, she realized that I was staring at her. "Are you okay?" she asked me.

I told my mom that I wasn't ok! I asked her, "Will grandpa be okay? Is he going to walk again?"

My mom nodded and said, "Yes, he is going to get better. You will see."

Then, she went to talk to her papa. "Papa, what is going to happen to you never walk again?" Said my mom.

"Mi hija, Juana, don't worry. I will be fine. I just need to rest."

"Papa, I promise you that I will work hard so I can pay the rent and buy food I will help out more."

"Mija , you don't have to do all that for me," he said.

"Ok papa, tell me, what happened to you? How did you end up like this?"

"Well, what happened is that I tried to pick up a box of fruits and I fell down."

"Next time, be careful, papa," said my mom.

And sure enough, over time he slowly started to heal and my mama did not have to take care of the whole family. And one day, she met my dad. Soon after, my mom and my dad got married. And, not long after that, they decided they should immigrate to the United States. They dreamt about it, and stared planning their trip.

But before they could make the voyage, my mom started feeling weird. She wanted to throw up when she ate any type of food. When she called my *abuela*, my *abuela* told her "Mija you are pregnant."

My mom was excited, happy, and surprised. My mom called my dad and told him all about it. So, the United States had to wait.

They had a baby, my brother. They loved him and took care of him and when my brother grew up, they decided that it was now time to come to United States. My mom decided to come separately when my brother turned two years old. My dad had already gone ahead to set up our home. He was already in United States, waiting.

When my brother turned three, my mom was crying and sad. She wondered whether she should leave him behind for a while because she was scared that she would lose him while crossing the border. But in the end, she took him with her. When they were crossing, my brother wandered off and he got lost.

My mom searched and searched. She cried and yelled. She felt hopeless. She returned to her parents, scared and alone. Then, she received a random call from a person and they told my mom that they found my brother. He was on the ground, in the dessert, dead.

My mom started crying and screaming and trying to kill herself when my dad called. "He is with me," he said. She was able to make sure that my brother was with him and she was happy, and joyful that both of them were together.

The next day, it was my mom's turn to cross the border. My mom was happy and sad at the same time. She was sad to leave my *abuela* and *abuelo,* but happy that she would see her husband and son. "*Mija,* be happy with your beautiful family and God bless you and your family, *Mija*. Be safe," said my *abuelo*.

"I want you to be happy and I want you to take care of yourself," said my *abuela*." "Thank you for all your hard, it was hard when I got hurt and you..." said my a*buelo*.
"I love you and god bless you, *Mija*," he added.

"Thank you papa," said my mom.

"*Mija,* please take care of my grandson and enjoy your life with your family. You are lucky you have a chance to have a better life for you and your family, take care *Mija.*"

"Thanks mama, thanks!" she said!

In the end, my mom made it. She lived happily in Los Angeles with my dad and my brother. And after I was born, she taught me that the secret to life is to live happily, no matter what happens, and always have a smile on your face. My mom was happy that she was able to provide her kids with a better life, and that is what is important.

The Day I Left to America

By: HA

"MOM, I AM SCARED!" I screamed. "Can we go back home with the family?"

"Sweetie, it's ok, do not worry. Everything will be fine." My mom said to me.

We were dirty and smelly. I was very tired. Each person in our group had there own water bottles and they had to make it last a week. I remember when I was done with my water bottle. I asked my mom if I could have some more water, but she did not have any either.

By the way, my name is Stephanie, and I am ten years old. This is my life, my life when I was little. I came to America when I was 8 years old, with my mom. My mom wanted to help my grandma and grandpa build a house because we lived in a shack made of wood, wood my grandpa found on the streets. So, my mom wanted to help my grandpa build a house.

My mom one day told me that we should go to America I told my mom, "No I want to stay here in Mexico where our family is."

"But we can help them more from the other side!" She said.

When I thought about it for a little longer, I told my mom,

"Mommy, you were right we have to go to America because we need to help *abuelito and abuelita* and you haven't been able to do that from here."

The next week, we said, "Goodbye" to our family in Mexico.

I told my grandpa, "Don't worry about us because we will be fine!"

When we got to Tijuana my mom and I waited for some people called *los coyotes*.

They threatened us. "If you get caught, don't tell anybody who brought you here to The United States! Do you understand?"

My mom nodded.

He gave us each a water bottle and we started to walk. It was really hot during the day. And at night, we slept in dug out holes, hidden by rocks. Sometimes we slept wherever the night came. When we were finally ready to make the final crossing, there was a helicopter, lights on, trying to find us.

We all started running as fast as we could. I was really tired, gasping and sweating. When we escaped from the helicopter we went to sleep again. The next day we got up and we walked a little more and on this final day, we got to America.

We waited for a car to pick us up, but the car did not come. We waited and waited and waited, thinking we had been abandoned, until the car finally appeared. We thanked God for sending us the car, which took us to a house and fed us.

From this strange house, my mom called my aunt.

Los coyotes grabbed the phone from my mom and told my aunt," If you want to take her, you have to pay. Bring money!"

My aunt did as she was told. She paid and they let us go. She took us to her big house and gave us a bed to share. We both fell asleep and slept for a long time. I could not believe that I was in America. My mom was so tired that she woke up at one in the afternoon, the day after we had gotten to my aunt's. As she was waking up, she was smiling. "Dream," she whispered, "And follow it, and if you follow it, your dreams will come true."

"Thank you for everything," I whispered, realizing we had made our dreams come true.

A New Home

By: PM

In El Salvador my family would always have fun because we would always have the family together. They would always celebrate birthdays and holidays making their delicious food, dancing all night, and laughing. Everything was a good.

My dad would always tell me stories about El Salvador how amazing it was, he would also tell me how good the food over there tasted. He would always plant beans and grow fruit.

Both of my sisters were born in EL Salvador and my brother and my little sister and I were born here in America. As my sisters were growing up, my mom decided to move to America, to have a new start because El Salvador was increasing in danger and my mom had no choice but to move to safety. It was hard for my mom to tell my grandma that they were leaving, but she did.

My grandma said to my mom, "I understand. You want to keep your kids safe."

My mom replied, "I'm going to miss you, mom and I will send money to you guys so you can buy what you want."

My sisters asked my mom, "Can we stay with grandma and grandpa?" My sisters didn't want to leave because they loved it there. So, they stayed.

As the days passed, the day arrived when my parents would leave. It was hard to say goodbye to their loved ones. The emotions that were in my parent's faces, the tears dripping of sadness off my mom's face from her eyes. They said goodbye to my grandparents, my cousins, my aunties and uncles, and my sisters and she told them, "Be good, and do whatever your grandparents tell you to do, I'll miss you." My sisters replied, "We will and we'll miss you too."

My parents grabbed their bags and my uncle took them to the airport and the plane that would take them to the United States. When they came to United States everything was perfect. They found a new home, new friends, new jobs, and a better life.

As time passed, my parents were thinking of bringing my sisters to the United States and live with them but my sisters didn't want to leave. My mom wanted them to come because she wanted to be with my sisters. Only one of my sisters came, and my other sister stayed. My sister wanted to cry but at the same time she was excited to see my mom.

When my mom saw my sister, my mom said, "Welcome to our home, my daughter." As they arrived at the house, they unpacked my sister's bag, showed her the room where she would be sleeping. She loved it, and hated it at the same time. She missed El Salvador and our grandparents. She missed our other sister, but she loved the five month old me. She wanted to go to school, but was also scared. Since she only knew how to speak

Spanish she thought that she was going to humiliate herself. The life of an immigrant is not easy, happiness and sadness go hand in hand as families are broken and reshaped.

El Salavador

By: RA

El Salvador is a busy country because you have to work hard to raise your kids. Also, it's a great country, well in most places, and it depends where you live because there are gangsters there that don't have a heart so they just kill people and they don't care.

Some people work hard to take care of their kids so that their kids can get ahead in life, so that their kids don't end up on the streets. Parents want the best for their kids, they want them to have a good job and a good life.

My cousin lives in El Salvador. She stayed in 6th grade for two years because she wouldn't do her homework or anything in class. She finally told me that she passed 6th grade and now she is in 7th grade.

My other cousin, Rafael, also lives in El Salvador. He is an amazing cousin. He is taller than me and always gives me advice. He tells me to study and to have a good career. He always tells me that if he had a chance he would come to the United States because in El Salvador he said that there are no job opportunities for people. Although he goes to school, he doesn't want to go anymore because with or without it, the best job he could ever find would pay him $5 a day.

Another reason why Rafael want's to come to the United States is because he wants the best conditions for his life and he told me that if he was here he would study because he is still underage. He knows that studying here and graduating high school would help him find a job. The jobs here would pay him enough to survive and save money to help bring his mom and his sisters. All he wants to do is support them and get his family ahead. He wants them away from the gangsters and worry of death.

Mexico

By CJ

In a quiet cold town, in Mexico, there were barely any people. I was in my room and my papa came in and the room filled with his cologne. His green shirt and black sweatpants caught my eye.

He approached me and when he did he said while stroking my hair "Mija, we're going to America. We are leaving Mexico today." The second he finished that sentence his voice sounded so low his eyes looked tired from working all night.

I said, trying to sound happy, "ok."

I looked up at him with a weak smile. I sat up straight and took a deep breath and my papa said, "*Disculpé mi hija linda*, excuse me my beautiful daughter, but we have to leave. My job isn't paying me that much. The jobs over there, in America, are better. I could become a doctor like I wanted to be, but here I'm just a chef at *La Casa de Pupusas*."

I let out a small giggle and papa smiled. He said, "Anyways we have to go Jas, we can't live like this anymore."

I frowned and nodded "I understand, papa" I said with a smile.

"*Te amo mucho*, I love you a lot," he said.

I smiled and said, "Me too."

As we finished packing I zipped my suitcase and pulled my hair back. I was a smart child back then, I knew what was going on around me. My papa came in with two bags hanging down his shoulders. He looked exhausted. I smiled and picked up my big bag and slouched, "Let's go papa."

I called my mom and my brother to make sure they were ready. I walked to her room with my little tired feet and checked on her. I peeked in "mommy, brother we're ready, are you?"

She zipped her case with force "*Vámonos, Mija*, let's go, daughter," she said and we rushed out the door. My parents were both excited, but I was crying my eyes out. I told myself while growing up that I would never leave Mexico, but here we were, leaving forever, going to another place where I've never been to before. My parents stood on either side of me, my mom on my right and my dad on my left.

It was a cold night. We weren't able to reach our flight on time. We were exhausted from all the walking, the airport is far from where we live and my noodle arms were tired.

My mom asked me while taking my bag out of my hand, "You tired, *Mija?*"

I nodded, so she took the bag from my hand and I took a big breath and exhaled.

My dad put the suitcases down and picked me up.

"Even though we missed our flight, we can't give up yet.

We've come so far, we can't turn back now," said my mom.

I rubbed my sleepy eyes and listened to what my dad said, "We're not turning back, ever! We'll walk all the way to America if we have to... no regrets."

I accidentally fell asleep. I felt like I was on the ground and I felt warm. I slowly opened my eyes and I saw darkness all around me. I looked over to one side and my mom was sleeping. On the other side, with my bag in between us, my dad and brother were also asleep. I yawned and went back to sleep.

I awoke from my sleep when I heard men shouting and boots sliding across the ground. I slowly opened my eyes to find that neither my mother nor father were around. I looked on the other side and saw my brother. I sat up quickly and looked around. I saw a huge truck filled with men in uniforms. My parents were in the back of the truck. The men were slamming the truck doors. My parents had tears falling down their faces. I tried to wake up my brother, but he wouldn't open his eyes. I stood up fast and tried to yank the bars open to free my parents, I was worried sick!

Someone grabbed my arm and threw me down. I looked up at the man and he said, "Sorry, Mija, but your parents can not pass!"

I screamed out while crying, "Why?"

The man grabbed my arm again and shook me, "Look kid,

your parents are illegally passing, we don't accept people without there're documents."

I dropped my jaw, "WHAT ARE YOU TALKING ABOUT? MY DADDY HAS EVERYTHING!"

They took my dad out and they grabbed him and threw him on the floor. I ran to him but the man put his arm out to stop me.

"Stay back!" He untied my dad's hands and yelled out "Show em!"

My dad looked up at the man and said, "Show what?"

The man said, "The documents! Take them out!!"

I was scared. My brother woke up and walked in front of me, protecting me. He yelled, "Hey, give us back our parents!"

The man said, "I'm just making sure your father and mother have their documents."

I yelled out, "They do have them. If he doesn't have them on him, then we have them in the suitcase!"

He again grabbed my dad and tied him back up and threw him in the back of the truck, beside my mom. I ran to the truck and tried yanking the bars open, but they were so strong. They were made of steel. My brother grabbed my waist and took me off the truck and I felt my heart rip to shreds and I cried and felt pain in my chest, as if my lungs were filled with knives. My brother hugged me. He rubbed my back as they drove off with our parents.

My brother whispered, "It's ok Jas, we'll get them back."
I saw my brother shed some tears as he said, "Hey, don't worry.
I'm still here, ok?" He got down on one knee and when h got to
my height, he touched my shoulder.

"It's ok...mom and dad are just heading back home. We'll
make it to America, just the two of us, I'll take care of you Jas."

I smiled weakly and said, "Let's go then."

"We have to change our plans. We can't fly there, so we
will have to walk" he said. And, we set off.

As we walked for 3 hours my stomach growled. I pet my
small tummy I said, "I'm hungry."

My brother looked down at me and said, "Ugh, Jas, please
don't start."

We walked and walked and walked. We worried about
our parents and walked some more. When we were just a few
days away from crossing the border. I collapsed. My face hit the
ground. I couldn't take it anymore. I was so tired from walking
that my little feet were aching. My brother helped me up. I
cleaned my bloody nose. My leg was stiff and I was limping like
a zombie.

Ever since the soldiers took our parents, it's been
different, quiet. We felt as if we were all alone, walking by
ourselves for miles until we saw… a village. I was thinking out
loud, *if we could stay here and find some help we could find mom
and dad faster...but sadly we don't know these people we don't*

know where they've been they could be a clan of horrible people.
Before I could say anything out loud, my brother took my hand walked me away.

"I don't wanna go down there!" I muttered when I realized where he was heading.

My brother looked down at me, "You're not the boss here, I am, now we're going down to that house!" I was angry with him for forcing me to do something I didn't want to do. He gripped my wrist tightly until I felt pain and fought back.

"You're mean," I said. I hit him with my fist. I didn't hit hard.

My brother gently grabbed my wrist and said, "Hey, don't ever do that again! I was upset. I started tearing up. We always go through this. I wanted to hit him when he took his anger out on me. He said, "God, you're so annoying. No wonder mom wants to get divorced with dad, it's all because of you!"

My heart and stomach dropped, I tried making it look like as if I weren't afraid. I said, "Well daddy told me that he doesn't love you!"

As we stood their fighting, we heard a car pull up. We hid downslope, beside a rock. It was the soldiers that took our parents, they were back, and our parents were with them.

My brother squeezed my hand and whispered, "Start running!"

I looked at him and asked, "Why?"

He whispered even louder "Just please go. Look, I'm sorry about what I said earlier, ok? I never meant it and it's not true, I was just upset and took it out on you"

I apologized as well, "I'm sorry too."

He gave me a tight hug. I grabbed his hand and started running. Behind us we could hear gunshots.

We heard screaming, "SHUT UP, YOU BAG OF TRASH!"

We ducked again behind a rock. We sat against it listening to the shouting and gunshots. We sat there for hours and the soldiers were still there screaming at their "prisoners." The whole road was full of them.

We had no choice but to ask for help from the villagers below. I pulled his sleeve and pointed downward. We reached the villagers and found the most innocent looking villager we could find, an old woman sitting on a bench. We asked, "Do you know another way out of this area?"

The old woman said, "No, I'm afraid not...but there is an underground sewer? You can use that, if you want," she smiled "but why do you need to escape?"

My brother pointed at the soldiers. The old woman looked scared, she added, "Oh, I escaped those horrible men too."

My brother's face was confused he said, "But how did you..."

The old woman replied, "I was smart and escaped!"

We were so confused. The old woman asked again, "Do you have your documents?"

We nodded.

The old woman replied, "Then what are you doing here? Shouldn't you be on the other side by now?"

"Yes, of course but the soldiers took our father and mother away. They were going to show them our papers, but they just kept yelling and shoving," I added.

"Oh! That's very strange...are you sure your father had papers?"

"Well, no. He told us right before we left the house, but he never showed us"

My brother looked at me and asked, "Do you think dad left them at the house?"

I said, "I think so, let's go back to make sure."

We left the old woman and returned home. We searched everywhere in our house, and finally found papers under my father's bed.

"Wait, I thought mom and dad said they had them...did they lie to us?" My brother asked.

I shrugged my shoulders, "Maybe they forgot," I said. "Let's go get our parents!"

Somehow, we made it back to the truck where the soldiers were. We held up the documents. My brother yelled out, "STOP, WE HAVE THE PAPERS! NOW GIVE US BACK OUR

PARENTS!"

After checking the documents, they released mom and dad to us. And together, as a family, we finally reached the border. We were exhausted and hungry, but we were together. My dad put his arms around us and said, "Thank you for saving your mother and I! We owe you one!"

I said, "Mommy, daddy, you don't owe us anything, we're just glad that we're all together again!"

My Life as an Immigrant

BY: ME

When I was born I had many challenges, like getting injured in my eye. It was scratched by a chicken nail and swelled. My mother and father began arguing about me see. My mother said, "I think we should let her die."

However, my dad said, "NO!, I won't let her die, I will call someone that can help her and that can save her life."

A doctor came and fixed my eye and my parents gave him all the money they had. My dad continued to sell food and clothes to make money. I didn't have enough time to do my homework, because as I got older, I helped my family by growing food. When I did go to school, the teacher would hit me with a big thick ruler and pour cold water on me while everyone watched. At home, the wild dogs would chase and bite me. Life was hard.

After many years, I finally got married to a wonderful man. We waited for the right time to leave our home and find a better life. Then, one night, we said goodbye to our families and traveled a long way to get to America. We overcame many dangerous challenges to get to America. The weather was too hot, the ground was too dry, and we only had 5 gallons of water. I didn't know how dangerous they really were until afterwards.

When we were tired, we rested for a while and then we kept on walking.

I had a wish that I should be free in another country and raise beautiful children.

I didn't know that I was going to have a baby until it was too late. The baby that was born was small and dead. He was gone forever. It was sad. I couldn't do anything. My life was ruined. I cried all day but my husband told me that our baby was in a better place and that god was now taking good care of him.

After 9 months, I had another baby. He was beautiful. He grew up and became smart. "I know that he will be special," I said. He turned 3 and I realized that I missed my parents. And soon after, I found out that I was going to have another baby, a boy.

I left work to take care of my children. My kids went to school in America. One day when my first son was in 2nd grade and my youngest son was in Pre-k, we stopped moving all the time. I wanted my sons to have friends.

We ended up in beautiful house where we had two more children, a girl and another boy. I took them to school and I fed them. I loved my family and I loved to cook for them, plus we got a wonderful dog for them to play with. *I had an wonderful life*, I realized. I only wished that my parents could see their grandchildren. Years have passed. My children grew up and traveled to Mexico to meet their grandparents. I was really happy that they took pictures of them and they went on adventures, but I also missed them because I hadn't seen them and I couldn't travel to Mexico to see them.

I learned a lesson from my children. I learned that everyone has dreams, to become someone or to do something that people have never done. You're able to do anything if you put your mind to it, just as I wanted to have a better life, my own children will one day make their dreams come true.

The Less Could be, More Successful

By: N J

In the city of L.A, imagine a mother that has three kids, but no husband, and it was really hard for her because there was a two-year-old baby. Imagine the struggles she experienced trying to feed me even though she had to feed the other two. I barely got milk because the rent was too much. But still I grew up healthy.

When I was growing up my mom was having some problems, but she didn't want to tell me about it. I heard her tell the neighbor that someone called her and said, "You are about to live on the street."

Then, the neighbor said, "Don't worry, someone is going to help you."

I was thinking to myself, *"Are we really going to live on the street?"*

I was going to ask my mom "Are you getting paid well?" *"What a dumb question!"* I said to myself, realizing that she would know that I was eavesdropping.

The reason why they were going to kick us out of our home was because the rent was way too much. The rent was about $950 and she was only receiving $400 dollars from the government and the rest she had to work, which only paid her $80 dollars a week. This was unfair because other people that cleaned houses got paid more. And the other reason it was unfair was because she cleaned very well and yet they still paid her 80 dollars a day. I knew this because my mom has been telling me the way she earned the money was by cleaning houses. I knew this because everyday my mom told me she was going to work, this made me feel sad because I couldn't spend time with her and I felt very lonely.

One day, my mom wasn't feeling well. She said, "My stomach is starting to hurt really bad."

I said to her, "Mom, are you going to feel better?"

But it was too late she had left already. Thankfully my uncle was there so they took her to the hospital. Once she was at the hospital the doctors just said, "She is going to need some surgery. Luckily we had just enough to afford the surgery for my mom. Finally, the doctor told us, "Your mother has cancer but it is possible for her to live."

I asked the doctor, 'What is it we can do in order to make my mom survive?'

He said, "She just needs surgery."

We were all very happy and we all said, "Thank you, Jesus Christ."

When the years went on. She was very happy for me because I was doing really good at school. Her eyes were filled with joy and happiness. Her voice said a million beautiful things that no one other than me could understand. But then something happened which made her very sad. She lost her loved one. She felt dead inside and outside. What she said was, "I am never going to feel the same in my life and I am never going to get help from anyone.

"This mattered to me because she isn't the same mom I knew for the past years. This mattered because things aren't going to be the same around our house. This mattered because she isn't going to be the strong and kind mom I knew, instead I am going to see her as a weak mom. But then she was in luck because her brother was moving in with us and she said "Finally we are going to get help from someone."

I asked, "Who?"

She said, "Your uncle."

We were all very happy because we not only had financial help, but we also got to have another man that can be with us. Ads the years went on and we were a very happy family. Then my uncle left to live in another house and my mom said, "Thank you so much for all the support."

So, the lesson I learned is that if you're ever in a tough situations, make sure that your family members are always by your side!

My Mother's Dreams Came True

By: MK

In Ipala, Guatemala, there was a family called Recinos. Where they lived, it smelled like wet fresh soil. The family Recinos owned a lot of territory. They planted there and sold their harvest. It was dusty there and calm where they lived. Their neighbors were very friendly. The Recinos family ate beans and tortillas everyday. They ate different foods but only on special occasions. Everyday was a happy day in Ipala. Everyone one lived happily there, except for one member of the family who wanted to cross the border, but why?

In Ipala, Guatemala the day was a gloomy and a windy. My mom worked in the fields *todos los seis días*, six days a week. My mom worked with my abuelito. My mama gets tired of working in the sun. Her hands were dusty and her fingernails got filled with dirt. My abuelito was used to it. My mom's two uncles also worked with my dad. Our house was very small. We shared one bed for each sister. Our floor was not a carpet, it was a dirt floor. We didn't have windows. We had a stove but we only used it for emergencies. Instead we used a campfire to cook.

My mom thought to herself, *"What if I cross the border to get to America?"* My mom was 27 years old then. Of course my mom's parents would not let her cross the border by herself.

My mom said, "I would be very happy if my parents allowed me to leave Guatemala because I want to have a new life and try a different job".

One month later, my oldest Uncle Moises was leaving Guatemala. He wanted to get to California. My mom was sad because her brother was leaving. They had good times together, but sometimes they fought too.

Moises told my mom, "I promise that I will find a better job and when you ask me for anything, I will get it for you."

"My brother Moises is very strong and he knows what to do," thought my mom. When he left, my grandma started to cry.

My mom held her hand and whispered, "Don't worry he will save us all."

By the way, my mom's name is Carmen Recinos. My mom was the 5th girl in the family, but then my mom's sister died when she was 5 years old. She died because she fell in the river and drowned.

My mom was very brave and strong and my mom thought positive thoughts. My mom dreamt dreams of going to California, but until her dreams could come true, she worked for my abuelo and helped by abuela.

Her days looked the same and went something like this: She fed the chickens in the morning. In the afternoon, my mom needed to get back to work with my dad. She knew that she needed to find the perfect time to tell her parents that she wanted to cross the border and get to America.

One night, as abuelita was cooking dinner, and we all sat together at the big table, praying before eating the food, she knew that she could not wait any longer. She would tell them that she wanted to go to America. Although, my mom felt a little nervous but knew that she needed to tell them because her dream was to go to America.

"Mom, dad, I need to tell you something," said my mom.

"What is it, hun?" said my *abuelita.*

"I ...I...I want to go to America"

Silence filled the room.

"I want to have a better job and a better future and I want to be with Moises," she said.

"You're too young to cross the border," said my *abuelita.*

"But my dream and life is over there."

"ENOUGH OF THIS DISCUSSION!" Said my *abuelito.*

After they finished their food, my mom and aunt washed the dishes.

"Why do you want to go to America?" Asked my youngest Tia?

"I want to go to America because … I don't know…" said my mother.

"Then, if you don't know then, why are you going to

America?" She asked my mother.

My mother could not answer. She did not know the answer.

"Answer me!" Said her younger sister. "You're not going to tell me?"

"Stop, I don't want to talk about it," said my mom.

After days and weeks of my mama working in the fields, she became exhausted. After she got home my mama needed to warm the tortillas before dinner, to help abuela. As everyone was seated for dinner, it was calm, and no one was talking during dinner. As everyone finished eating their food they all were preparing to go to sleep.

My mom heard my *abuela* and *abuelo* talking in their room. My mom couldn't hear what *abuela* and *abuelo* were talking about. After she changed into more comfortable clothes, she went to see what they were talking about.

"We were thinking that you were right about crossing the border to get to America," said *abuela,*

"We don't want you to have a horrible life in Guatemala so that is why we have decided that it is time to make a decision. if you want to go to America, you have our permission. You can go," said *abuelo.*

"We are all going to support you and hope that your trip to America is safe," said *abuela.*

"Really? You will do that for me?" Said my mother.

"And I promise that I will contact Moises," said my mom.

Two weeks later my mother had the day off of working in the fields. My *abuelo* went to Ipala to go to church. My *abuela* and her daughters were at home making dinner. My mother was making the tortillas.

"What are we making, mama" said my mom.

"We are going to cook chicken soup" said *abuela.*

"SENORA, SENORA, SENORA!!!!!!" Said a man, panting desperately.

"Que paso, what happened?" Said my *abuela.*

"Senor Antonio, your husband was involved in a car accident!" Said the man.

"WHAT? We have to go to Ipala," said *abuela.*

The rest of the daughters stayed at home and *abuela* went to get a taxi with the man. All the sisters started crying and the youngest son was upset and scared. Later my Uncle Moises came to Guatemala and went to the hospital. My mom started to pray and she stared at the night sky.

Abuela came to the hospital, trying to find out more information from the nurse. She entered and she started crying because she didn't want to see her husband connected to different cords and machines. He was asleep, but she started to talk to him.

The next day, they operated on him and afterwards, as he lay in bed, trying to wake up, *abuela* sat besides him. He started to eat, a little bit. My *abuela* contacted her kids to tell them that my *abuelo* was alive. It took a week to get him strong enough to go home, but he finally did.

My mama went to his room and talked to her parents. They were talking about the future, her future. Her parents weren't sure whether she should go to America just then or wait a while because of my *abuelo's* accident.

My mom understood, she said she would wait until the time was right. Instead of dreaming about the future, she made chicken soup for him and helped in the fields. The week went quickly for my mom.

And after *abuelo* recovered, she prepared to leave. She was excited and scared at the same time, scared of the immigration police. She packed up all her things. My *abuelita* prayed for my mom's safe crossing.

They all ate a good dinner. My *abuela* made *carne asada* with *chile, frijole,* and *arroz.* Everybody loved meat, chile, beans, and rice. My mom needed to sleep extra early to wake up at 4.am.

She was going to wake up before the sun came up so that she could cross the border. She changed into a flannel, jeans, and tennis shoes. My mom was going with a group of people and a family member. They all met up in a place where the police couldn't find them.

"*HOLA*, hello, CARMEN," said Pauola, her distant

family member.

"*Hola*, hello," said my mom.

"How are you?" said Pauola.

"Fine," said my mom even though she was extremely nervous.

The entire group started to walk. They were all happy and talking together. In the group there was a man in charge. They all talked over his plan, which was a path they would take so that the police would not catch them.

My mom walked in the back of the group, carrying a big bottle of water. The big water was very heavy, and the job was hard, but she did it anyway. They were walking in silence when suddenly…

"HE IMMIGRATION POLICE ARE HERE, EVERYONE RUN!!!!" said a man.

Everyone started running. My mom couldn't because she was holding the big container of water. She was lost and couldn't find her group. The helicopter cast it's light on my mom.

My mom was super scared because she didn't want to get caught. Then the helicopter just left, as if it had never even seen them. So, they didn't caught. She was relieved, but also scared. During this experience, the group got scattered. My mom was alone, in the desert. My mom was walking miles and miles looking for her group. Suddenly she heard a group of people chatting. She went over and the man who was in charge said,

"Are you lost?"

"Yes," said my mom.

"Do you want to stay with us?" Said the man.

"Where are you guys going?" Asked my mom.

"California… are you going there?" Asked the man.

"Yes… I'm going there," said my mom.

"Alright you can stay with us," said the man.

And, she did.

They walked and walked, and after walking for a long time, they took a break. The day was about to be over. The group found a place to stay. They stayed there and they ate dinner and chatted a little. The man who was in charge had contacted my *abuelo* and asked for more money to take my mom across. My *abuelo* was a little nervous and scared but then he had lots and lots of hope, he agreed to the man's terms. Everyone was sleeping, also my mom. Nobody heard any of this.

The next day the group was packing their stuff to go to their next stop. Everyone was eating while they were walking. It was a sunny day and everyone was sweating. Everyone wore clothes they could camouflage in. They were covered from head to foot. My mom was so covered that you could only see her eyes.

After walking for six days, they neared the Guatemalan airport. The man who was in charge of the group went to the airport. He talked to the people who worked in the airplane. All of a sudden he came back with papers and gave it to the people in the group, even my mom.

"Thank you for everything," said my mom

"*No problema*," said the man. "Well, I have to go back and bring another group of people," said the man.

"Do you know what happened to the other group I was with?" Said my mom.

"The other group was caught by the immigration policie" said the man.

"Oh, okay, I hope my cousin is okay," said my mom.

"I hope so too," said the man.

"Okay, bye," said my mom.

"Bye!!" said the man

My mom entered the plane with her fake papers. They let her pass without a word and showed her to her seat. She closed her eyes and waited, waited to open them again and be in California.

When she got to California, my Uncle Moises was waiting with his wife and daughter, Sandy. She was happy to see her brother again. She moved in with them and one day, two months later, she found a job, cleaning a house.

She was a hard worker. Since she didn't know how to drive a car, she used a bus to everyday to get to where she needed to go. Over time, she met some friends and she talked with them.

They shared their stories and my mom shared hers.

Her friends were not happy, so my mom had a lesson for them. Her lesson was, "If you want something then earn it, and how do you earn it, by working hard!" Her lesson was so powerful that her friends nodded and said that it was all, true. Her friends became hard workers too, just like my mom.

Later, after I was born, she shared this story with me too. I realized that my mom was a special person. She wanted me to have an education and reach my goals. She wanted me to go to a University and earn an education. She is a good person who wanted to get to America. This story is about my mom's life and her life's journey.

A Small City

By: MA

In a small city called La Capital, in Guatemala, a family of four lived in a big house full of love. The young girl, the oldest in the family (ME), imagined herself in the future. She also imagined herself spending time with her mom and her dad. She also had many other dreams, where she would grow to become a dancer and a singer. She also imagined her life being perfect with her beloved parents and her brothers.

One day, the young girl's dad looked at his daughter and told her he would give her the world and everything in it. He wanted to see her dreams come true, to see her as a dancer, and a singer, but instead he told the little girl, "You have to promise me that you are always going to protect your family and protect your mother with all of your heart." The young girl was confused with what her dad was trying to tell her, but she nodded and swore to herself that she would keep the promise.

That night, the little girl couldn't sleep, she kept on thinking about what her dad had told her. She asked herself *"Why would my dad tell me this?"* She had no clue what was coming her way!

The next day, the little girl woke up early and went

outside. She didn't know why, but she felt more relieved because she could feel herself thinking through the thoughts when she was outside. She thought of her father and how he was trying to tell her what he was feeling. What she didn't notice was that her dad was there too, gazing at her. Little by little, she started slowly tearing up, she thought to herself, *"What would I do without my parents?"* The little girl didn't understand why she had felt like this, but she knew that she would be okay if she could just forget about it.

Three weeks later her abuelita called her mother to tell her that she was going to finally come for a visit. Her mother was so surprised that she burst out with tears. She was so confused about why her mother was crying, so she stood next to her and put her arms around her body. Her mother looked at her daughter and told her, "I have never been more excited in my life."

She asked her, "Then, why are you crying?"

Her mother smiled with tears in her eyes and told her the good news, "Your abuelita is finally going to come and see you. Also, I haven't seen her since I was 13 years old."

This was a magical moment for both mother and daughter. She was glad to finally meet her abuelita, but most importantly she was happy to see her mother as happy as she was. At the same time she felt relieved that nothing bad had happened to anyone and that her mother's tears were tears of joy.

One week passed and her grandmother was an hour away

from the house. The little girl was excited, but nervous. The little girl's mom was also glad that she was going to see her mother again; she had even stayed up the whole night, cooking and cleaning, because she couldn't wait.

The time came, the time they were all waiting for, the time when... everything went silent. Grandmother was near. Her mom called the airport and asked if the flight to Guatemala had landed and some woman on the other end said, "Yes." The family was all confused because abuelita should have gotten there an hour before but was late.

Mother stayed awake another night, worried about abuelita. The next morning the girl woke up to a sound and smell of eggs and beans heating on the stove. She had quickly got up and ran to the kitchen, she knew what the sound was. It was the sound of abuelita's cooking. She screamed as loud as she could and ran to her grandmother. They spent an amazing month together, eating, laughing, and telling stories. Life was perfect.

Sooner or later the time came, the time that grandmother had to say her goodbyes and go back to Guatemala. That morning did not go as planned, it was quiet and everyone had tears in their eyes. The girl cherished spending time with grandmother. The moment that grandmother left, the girl remembered her dad's words, "...protect your family and protect your mother with all of your heart." As she saw her mother's tears rushing down her face, the girl knew that something bad was going to happen, something that was out of her control, something that would cause her not to keep the promise to her father.

When the little girl turned 5, a few months later, she new that something bad was about to happen. The little girl's birthday party ended, but her dad never showed up. That night, the little girl got into bed and started to cry she heard her parents arguing and screaming at each other. As she tried to cover her ears and tried to stay positive in her imaginary world, she couldn't help but wonder where he had been? Why they were now fighting?

A few days later, the time had come, the little girl's mom dropped. She had received the bad news...

"He died?" she said.

The little girl had felt a pin drop in her heart and in that moment she felt dead inside. She didn't need to ask, *"who?"* She knew. Deep inside, she knew whom her mother was talking about. The little girls wished that she could get a chance to say goodbye or to at least hold him as close as possible one last time. Her mother, on the other hand, stopped talking. She had no words to describe what had happened, so she stopped talking altogether.

The day of his funeral, everyone gathered around to say his or her goodbyes to him. Once it was the little girl's turn to go up to his coffin, the first thing she did was grab her father's hand and put it against her heart. As her father's hand was against her heart she studied all the flowers around her father's coffin. As she took a deep breath she smelled a strange smell, and knew that the flowers were just there to hide the smell of death and mask their fears. As the little girl kneeled down and said her prayers, she felt a final connection, she didn't want to let go, she knew that she wouldn't have a chance to see him ever again.

She kneeled there for half an hour. No one bothered her or tried to pull her away. No one told her anything; she just knelt there and stared at her father. Then, suddenly she thought, *"How can I survive without him?"*

She felt her mother's hands on her shoulders, pulling her back, pulling her out of the darkness. It was time to bury her father in the ground, the little girl didn't want to let go, but her mother's hands would not let her go.

She new that her father had left and she only had his coffin now. The last thing she remembered of the coffin was that it was white and that he lay in it, clutching a note she had put under his hand.

The little girl talked to the coffin as she had to her father once, "I will take care of mother and brother!"

"I will never let you down!"

"I will never let anything break me or this family down."

As she walked away from the coffin she exploded into tears. She looked back to her dad and she wondered what life would be like now. She knew that her mother needed her more than anything, because she was the first child.

As the girl stood next to her mother, she whispered, "It is all going to be okay, mom, as long as we stick together."

Her mother smiled and responded with tears dripping down her face and told her, "Your dad would be so proud of you!" She hugged her daughter tightly and added, "He will always have a special place in our hearts."

Although her dad passed away, she tried to stay positive and be the best leader for her brothers. She lived in a small apartment with her mother and her two brothers and she learned young, never to give up, and always to keep one's head up.

When her youngest brother was old enough, she pulled him aside and told him the same things her dad had told her, "You need to promise me that we will protect this family and protect mother once I leave and have children of my own."

He nodded and to this day, even though he now has children of his own, he has kept the promise he made his older sister all those years ago.

Tragedy

By: TB

At a young age, I wasn't living a lovely life like most kids do nowadays. I didn't have a fancy phone, not even a flip phone (people back then didn't even know what a flip phone was, it didn't exist). I didn't have 10 pairs of shoes like others did. I only had 2 pairs of shoes a year, one pair for home and another pair for school. At least, in my time, there was better communication between people then there is today.

My name is Esperanza and this story is about a time long past, when I was only 10 years old. My older sister was 14 years old, only four years older than I was. My mother's name was Margara. My father's name was Abraham, neither of whom I'd seen for years. I was living with my grandmother, and older sister and we had decided that enough was enough; we were going to go find our parents and nothing would stop us.

The house I lived in was rusty, and small. Maria, my older sister and I would sleep in a room with two beds. Both of our beds were old, super dirty and we only had one blanket, so we cut it in half one for her and the other half for me. Even though the house wasn't the best you have ever heard about, we were glad because we had shelter and wouldn't have to sleep outside, in the wind where you would see trees roughly moving from left to right.

One day, I was walking home from school and unexpectedly I heard gunshots. I ran as fast as I could but I tripped on a rock, scraped my knee and twisted my leg. Blood started coming out non-stop. I realized that a part of my leg got paralyzed but I couldn't stop just there.

I tried hiding in between two houses with peelings of paint coming off but my foot steps covered with blood made it simple for someone to find me, either way I stayed as quiet as possible. I was sitting down on the dirt floor with shattered glass everywhere. My head was facing down touching one of my knees, while my eyes filled with tears. I looked at one of my bent legs, numb.

Suddenly, I heard one of the crackling of glass. I knew that somebody was approaching. I looked at the person's shoes. They were black and it looked like his shoe size was around a 9 ½. I looked up and saw his broad shoulders and his muscular arms holding the biggest gun I had ever seen. His deep voice said "GET UP!"

So, I did. But then, I realized that he wasn't talking to me. He was talking to another man, a buffer man. This random man said to the buff man, "Hey, over here!"

My vision was getting blurry every time I blinked. I wasn't able to see clearly what the man was holding in his hand,

63

but it distracted the guy with the gun so I took advantage and limped away from both men.

The day was darkening. Most houses I saw were vacated. I didn't have a choice so I went inside one of the many abandoned house. Layers of dirt were lying on the floor and in the windows. I walked in and looked around the house to try finding a good spot to hide. I saw a string hanging from the ceiling in the upstairs room, I pulled it carefully and a ladder came down. I climbed up. The first thing I saw was a dusty box in the left side of the room.

On the right side of the attic there was items people probably didn't need or hadn't used in a long time. There was chairs, drawers, big poles and all of those materials had dust and dead spiders covering them. After I fully got inside of the attic I slowly went to open that box.

My hands were shaking. Something in the right side of the attic was moving. I tried to push the box to the corner of the wall. It was heavy, but I was able to get it to the corner of the left wall. I was scared to open it but I had no choice, how was I going to protect myself if there was nothing but that box in the left side of the attic.

Inside of that crusty box I saw an AK-47, with other different guns like a desert eagle, Thompson Uzi, and grenades. I got a gold Desert eagle pistol and it was heavy. I was distracted by all of those guns. The door from the attic closed fast and hard.

It scared me. Behind all of those drawers was a small girl. She was probably 6 years old. I was so close to shooting her because I was afraid it was one of the men I had run from. My heart was beating fast but I calmed down because I had someone younger than myself that was looking at my reactions. I gave her some pistols and grenades because I wanted her to protect herself too.

We heard footsteps we tried not to make noise. We could hear people walking around the house. All of a sudden we couldn't hear the footsteps anymore. Then they found the string and pulled it, so we quickly ran out through the window. We climbed down and ran as fast as possible, but the little girl couldn't run fast so I carried her. I had no idea where we were heading.

We got to this place where there was a lot of plants. The house in front of it was made out of bamboo sticks. We searched for more items to protect us from anyone bad and that's when we found a boat with 2 paddles in it. We turned it over and put it in the water. At first we thought it was a little pond that could at least get us from one side to the other. Passing all the plants and grass, we paddled as fast as we could. We heard gunshots and the men that we had heard earlier had found us and gathered up more people.

We were very close to reaching safety. The closer we got, I could read "Welcome to China," these men that had guns at the entrance said stop your boat. So we paddled 3 times as hard as we could and the guards threatened us. "If you don't go of the paddles we will shoot."

We let go and raised our hands up and the men that were chasing after us kept trying to shoot us but they didn't have a good angle since there was lots of rocks and the boat was moving fast. Within seconds we passed the border and were under Chinese protection. After that, the guards told the men, "You cannot shoot they are a part of us and if they are shot, you will have to suffer the consequences." So the men left.

Later on that night, the guards took us to a place where you could see a room nicely organized and we slept there for a couple of days. The last day we stayed there, we saw people injured and sick and in between them I had found my older sister. I was happy to know that I had a family member next to me.

"What are you doing here?" I asked her.

"I left Grandma's house, looking for you. I never thought I would see you again."

"But you did and together, we will find our parents!" I said.

It kept me calmer, having her around. Later, they gave us food and kept us alive. We then asked them if they could take us to the United States or tell us how to get there. They asked us to fill out paperwork and we were granted Asylum by the United States, which meant that they gave us permission to enter the country as documented immigrants, they even gave us money and helped us get into the country.

When we got there, we looked for a house or a place to stay in. We walked for hours and didn't find anything or anyone who wanted to help us, except for this girl around 16 years old lived with her uncle and her aunt. She took us to them and asked if we could sleep there for a couple of days, until we found a shelter of our own. The uncle took long to respond but said yes. We slept there for a couple of days. And the uncle and aunt's names were Lucas and Betty.

They told us, "We are here to offer you anything you want."

I said, "Thank you."

They asked me questions, "Do you have a mom or dad? What happened to you three?"

So, we explained. "Yes, we have a mom, but she left me and my dad to find a better job and send us the money. I had a dad too, but after my mom left, my dad got really sick and died. So we had to take matters into our own hands."

Lucas and Betty's faces were surprised as if they had never heard such an epic tragedy like mine. So they helped us find our mom. She cried when she saw us, but not tears of sadness, but instead she shed tears of joy. She had a smile on her face. The first thing she told both of us was, " I LOVE YOU!"

We explained to her what happened and eventually the little girl became a part of our family too.

Years passed and we were still a happy family. My mom, Lucas and Betty became very close family friends.

As my mother says, "At the end of the day your hair will be messy, your feet dirty, your eyes sparkling, and you will focus on the things that tear you apart or hold you together, but at the end there will always be love." Everything is possible when we are all United!

The Promise Land

By: SM

A long time ago, in a land far away, across the Pacific Ocean, stuck in between two continents, there lived a family of sixteen. The oldest, Chakh Mama and Metz papa were the king and queen of the family. They had four sons, who had wives, who also lived under their roof. And, each of the sons also had two kids each, except for Armen and Siran, who wanted children more than anything else in the whole wide world but had none for reasons I cannot and should not explain here.

This land they lived in was called Armenia and it was the happiest and saddest of places. It held memories but lacked food. And every year, for ten years before this story took place the family wanted to leave Armenia. They wanted to find a better land, a new home where there was plenty of food and opportunities.

"Why will this government not let us out?" one of their sons yelled.

"Maybe because it isn't time, Metz papa, would say. When it is time, then everything will work out without any problems."

Metz papa was right. Unfortunately, when it was time, he

was no longer in the picture. He had died a year before of a heart attack in his son Armen's arms and with his last breathe he said, "I wish one day that you will hold your own child and feel the love of father!"

They buried him behind the house, and planted plants over him, and sure enough exactly one year after his death, Armen and Siran had their first living-breathing child, Marine.

And on that day, a miracle happened, a letter came in the mail announcing, permitting, the family passage to a new land: Lebanon, a land of hope and opportunity, a land where they could provide for their children and live a respectable existence.

"Now? Now? Why now?" Asked Chakh mama, which means fat mama because she was large.

"Mama, this is what we've been waiting for!" Her sons exclaimed. They hugged each other and started to dance around their sitting room as though there was a band playing the happiest of songs.

"Armen and Siran just had a baby. Your father is dead. How am I going to get this family to Lebanon!" She exclaimed. She then crumpled, like a coat, onto the corner of her bed, since she slept in the sitting room the family used on a daily basis.

"You are not doing this alone, Mama." Her eldest boy said. "We will help you."

She did not speak. She did not get up. She lay on her bed, eyes closed.

"What is it?" Another son asked.

Then after many long minutes, she said, "How will we travel? How will we get sixteen people from Armenia to Lebanon? We don't have that much money."

"You want me to borrow money from…"

"No, we do not beg!" She said.

"Do you want me to rob a bank?"

She jumped up then and grabbed her son by the collar. "Just because your papa is no longer alive does not give you a right to say or do such stupid deeds! NO, NO, NO! We do not steal."

"Then what mama? What will we do?

She looked around the sitting room then, at the dirt floor, the old furniture; the faces of her sons, their wives, her grand babies, and then taking a deep breathe, she said, "I will sell this house. The money we will use to buy our air-faire. I will do what needs to be done.

And the very next day, she took the deeds to the house and the land and she walked to the town center where all the old buildings surrounded the beautiful water fountains, where young lovers held hands and walked, where children ran around eating ice cream cones. She knew that she would never see any of this again, but instead of stopping and running home, she entered the official building, asked to speak to an agent and handed her the paperwork.

"I want to sell the house, and the land. Give me as much money as it is worth. Do not try to cheat me or I will go elsewhere." She explained all this without getting mad, but sitting firmly and starting at the man across from her as if she were the man of the house.

She filled out paperwork, left her name, address, and information and did as she was told. For two months, she was told to check back next week, and every week, she was always sent away, until one week when she was not. That week, she was given more money than she had ever imagined.

She took the money and went to the jewelry store. She didn't ask anybody for permission. She was now the head of the family and she was the one that made the decisions. She carried the money close to her body, in a paper bag, scared that somebody would jump out of the shadows and snatch it away. She walked into the jewelry story and asked, "What can I buy with this money?"

They looked at her as if she were crazy. It wasn't every day that a woman walked in with thousands of dollars wanting to buy jewelry.

"Are you sure you want to do this?

"Certain." She said, and she patiently picked out four diamond rings, one for each of her sons, necklaces, bracelets, ear rings. She left enough money that would help pay for passage and traveling costs, but he rest of it she carried home as jewelry.

And this jewelry, they hid in the wraps of my blankets, as I was carried from Armenia to Lebanon.

"Nobody will want to check a screaming baby," she said.

"Everybody will think she is sick or tired, but nobody will suspect that she is carrying with her our hopes and dreams." Her sons agreed.

Nobody dared argue or second-guess Metz Mama.

"Do not hand her over for any reason," she cautioned her daughter-in-law.

And so the plan was set, the family would immigrate, reach out and grasp new dreams. Together, they would leave, and together they would remain! The day came quickly. Tickets were purchased. The house was evacuated. Everything was stuffed into suitcases they could carry or left behind forever.

In the end, after all of the family was saved, there was a lesson to be learned. Metz mama stood in front of her family, feet firmly planted on Lebanese land. She put her hands on her hips and she said, "There is nothing I wouldn't do for my family!"

This is the lesson she taught her boys, and this is the lesson they taught their children. This is the lesson my own papa taught me when I was growing up, for that baby, in wrapped like a stuffed grape leaf and carried from Armenia to Lebanon, grew up to be me, the writer of this story!

Grandpa Went Home

By: SS

In a far away land where people listen to the wind's song as it shadows threw the ground, people's sandals stomping on the ground while they walk to their destinations, older rustic house's catch people's eyes as they walk. In this land, I learned to adore my Grandpa.

My Grandpa once told me, when I was just a child, that these are the nights to remember. I asked, "Why did you say that?"

"You will understand the purpose of your life and know how to love life enjoy life before life ends you!" Grandpa said.

"Ok grandpa," I said with no idea about what he meant.

One day, Grandpa took me into his arms and said, "Think of me when ever you are afraid. I see both hope in your heart and broken arrows. Take my hand and don't let go." My eyes got watery. I hugged him like I was going lose him.

And one day, I did. I was waiting at the gate for Grandpa to come and pick me up from school so we could go home and eat. I waited and waited. I left the school to look for my Grandpa. I saw a man on the floor bleeding on the ground and his leg was shot. I came a little closer and saw the face of the man. It was my Grandpa. I saw him in pain so I called my mother and told her what happened to Grandpa.   My mother came in a hurry and called an ambulance.   Minutes later, I saw red lights flashing.   The paramedics came and helped my Grandpa get into the ambulance. My eyes started getting watery. I never wanted Grandpa to end like this.

March 24

My Grandpa always said things like, "Live a life that you will remember!"

When we finally got to the hospital they took him into operating room. I was terrified and tired. After hours and hours of waiting to see Grandpa, I fell asleep.

The next morning, I felt a pair of warm hands on me. It was my mom's hands. She was telling me to wake up, "Mija, wake up we have permission to see your Grandpa."

I groaned as I got up. We slowly walked to his room and when I walked in I saw my Grandpa connected to many machines. It was the worst feeling ever.

He finally woke up. I looked into his eyes. I saw deep love shining out. I stood next to my Grandpa as he looked at me. He took my arm and put his hand on my hand. A tear fell off my face and onto my hand as I just looked at him in pain.

The doctor had to come check on him.   The next the doctor helped him into a wheelchair. We took him outside. We were talking about how we wished we could run or go to the park, but then I asked Grandpa, "How did you come to the United

States?"

He said, "Well, I left my daughters, all 5 of them, to go to the United States… moving was hard. I took a bible, clothes, and I traveled by foot. I needed better work to be able to bring them here… umm it was hard, but I read every day in that train. I read that bible as if there are lessons in it on how to get to the Promised Land. I'll get there and thank God I did, I made it, then I found out that 2 of my oldest daughters were coming here too. Your mom was coming, you know, she crossed the border? We both finally got our papers and that's my story as an immigrant."

He said once again, "My child, live the beautiful life you have been given. Stretch for the stars!"

I replied, "What does that mean?"

"The star is your goal in life, reach for your goals."

The next day I got ready to go visit Grandpa again, but my mom told me we weren't going to the hospital because it was raining, flashing thunder in the sky. My mom and I stayed home for 2 days. While I was playing with my dolls, my mom got a call from the hospital; it was about Grandpa, something had happened, I'm not sure what, it had to do with his brain, he was alive, but he was not the same, ever again.

He's been in bed for a long time. It seems permanent. He can't move his shot leg, he has been in a coma on and off for weeks. When he finally woke up, I cried my eyes out, but I kept visiting him. He changed hospitals, but I always kept him in my heart.

We paid all his bills. I prayed to God every day of my life. I kept my faith hoping that Grandpa would one day come home. One Christmas Eve, we visited Grandpa and gave him a blanket. I talked to him the way he used to talk to me and wish he understood what I was saying. He just looked at me or past me.

Then he got worse. He had a heart attack, but they revived him. I cried tears of joy. A week later he had a stroke. I thought this was the end of his life, but he woke up the next day.

And when I finally graduated elementary school, I was so happy because I wanted to go show my grandpa my certificate. He tried giving me a smile, I think. We prayed before we left, like always.

On January 29th, 2015, after his second heart attack, Grandpa finally went home. He went to heaven. He doesn't suffer any more.

He was my biggest fan, the reason I am who I am. He taught me to appreciate life before life comes and ends you.

Forgotten

By: NA

Long ago in Mexico a boy was born, he grew. He was 13 when he met a woman named Ana. They met in school. As soon as he saw her he fell in love. She had on a nice dress, the color was a bright red with a nice shinny necklace so he thought that he could not talk to her because she looked like a girl that had money, so he didn't talk to her until she went to go and talk to him.

He was so shy he just left, running to his house without stopping once.

Finally he asked her to be his girlfriend.

She said yes!

She was his everything.

They got married.

They had 8 kids, three of them were boys and the other 5 were girls.

Now they only have two boys because the last one, he died. It was very sad when they found out that their last kid died. They felt a lot of pain. Years passed and they still were crying for the kid.

So when two of their other boys wanted to leave to

America, and they did, it broke their hearts.

They lived alone in Mexico, without their children, waiting, hoping that they would not be forgotten.

Acknowledgements

This compilation of stories allowed a class of scholars an opportunity to go home and talk to their parents about their shared history. An ethnographic study was conducted and stories were created out of it, giving the authors creative license to shape and mold the initial collected interviews.

As they researched similar stories and topics, their work transformed and they became tomorrow's activists. This compilation of stories is their way of "standing up and shouting out" about the struggles of all immigrants and sharing their awakened souls with their readers.

Due to the sensitivity of the topic, names have been omitted and changed to protect the author's and their families.

The team would like to thank Ms. Veda Smith for the opportunity she has given our team in sharing our voices and souls with the world. Another special shout out goes to Ms. Susan Weber who has collaborated with Ms. Smith in coordinating and making our dreams come true.

We would also like to thank Belen Terrones for the Graphic Design, which was used on the front cover of this book, without her illustration, our vision would not shine forth.